Selected Poems

Poetry Collections by Alan Sillitoe

The Rats and Other Poems (1960)
A Falling Out of Love and Other Poems (1964)
Love in the Environs of Voronezh and Other Poems (1968)
Storm and Other Poems (1974)
Snow on the North Side of Lucifer (1979)
Sun Before Departure (1984)
Tides and Stone Walls (1986)
Collected Poems (1993)

Alan Sillitoe

Selected Poems

Chosen By
Ruth Fainlight

First published in Great Britain in 2020 by Dare-Gale Press
15-17 Middle Street, Brighton BN1 1AL

www.daregale.com

ISBN   9780993331145

Printed and bound in Great Britain by TJ International, Padstow

CONTENTS

Introduction and 'The Motorway' by Ruth Fainlight

When Alan Sillitoe was awarded the European Poetry Prize* in Italy in 2008, his acceptance speech began:

> A novelist may hide his identity behind his fiction for the whole of his writing life, but in a poet's work lies the unconcealed emotional history of his heart and soul. A record, however seemingly disguised, cannot be falsified, supposing that the poems are true to himself, and what poems are not, if they are poems? The inner life is more discernible, though only after diligent searching, than any self-portrait in a story or novel. I became a writer, thinking myself more of a poet than a novelist. Poetry was more important than fiction. Though fiction has dominated me as a writer (perhaps to prevent me from ever being idle) I still think poetry is a superior means of expression than prose.

Like many young writers Alan began as a poet. We were in our early twenties when we met and each of us wrote more poetry than anything else. Poems and short stories: they both seem to originate in the same part of the brain, while novels come from a different area. It may seem odd that this happens: poetry perhaps being a more demanding craft than prose. But poetry is the more ancient form of literary expression and cadenced, rhythmic language seems to be the natural response to the pressure of emotion, whatever sort of emotion it is: love, anger, spiritual frenzy, any mental disturbance. Such intense feelings can also be produced by and be the response to what is called inspiration.

I cannot write about Alan's poetry in the objective, analytical, literary-critical way that would be possible with anyone else's work. We were too close, too involved in the shared life-experiences, ideas and influences, which surely were the source of some of our poems. Reading his poems for this selection, particularly the earlier ones, makes me remember where we were and what we were doing when he first showed me the draft which he thought sufficiently realised to be read by another person: and that person was me. We were each other's first reader and, certainly in my case, it was something that continued as long as possible, and which I have greatly missed since his death.

I have always admired the idiosyncratic style of Alan's poetry and the probably unique way his mind worked. Alan wrote poetry all his life and it was central to his work as a writer. He published seven volumes of verse during his lifetime as well as a *Collected Poems* in 1993 which also included new work. I have chosen the poems from each of these collections which are my personal favourites, but they also I think demonstrate the range and enduring value of his poetry. As well as being an extraordinary person, a master of the short story form and a wonderful novelist, Alan was a true poet.

*The European Poetry Prize is awarded annually by the Cassamarca Foundation in collaboration with the European Commission and under the aegis of UNESCO. It is awarded to a poet 'who has witnessed, in his or her work, the inalienable importance of a united Europe and its community values.'

The Motorway

I was born in the motorway era:
we both were. He used to say it made him
happy to see me writing in the car,
in the passenger seat.

We drove the motorways – going north on
the M1, all the routes through France heading south,
west from Nashville to San Diego, north
to San Francisco, then east again
across the continent to Montauk Point,
you driving, me writing.

Sometimes I'd be aware you'd quickly turned
your head sideways, only for a moment
shifting your gaze from the road – one flick
of your eyes, to watch me making notes.
I laughed and said: 'It's perfect: you driving,
me writing, let's go on like this forever,'
and you smiled and agreed.

But we didn't. There were other things to do.
And now it's impossible. You're dead.
And I'm driving with another person,
with someone else.

I stare through the windscreen into the distance
as the pylons draw their lines of power
across the green and brown and yellow fields,
the landscape of small hills, hedges and streams
you taught me to understand – stare into
the distance – as if by looking hard enough
I'll find that place where the two sides
of the road meet and unite.

Shadow

When on a familiar but deserted beach
You meet a gentleman you recognize
As your own death, know who he is and teach
Yourself he comes with flower-blue eyes

To wipe the salt-spray from all new intentions,
And kiss you on each sunken cheek to ease
Into your blood the strength to leave this life:
(A minor transmutation of disease)

To watch the mechanism of each arm
Inside your arms of flesh and fingernail,
To despise the ancient wild alarm
Behind each eye. Shaking your hand so frail

Your own death breathes possessive fire
(A familiar voice that no one understands)
Striding quickly, sporting elegant attire,
Coming towards you on these once deserted sands.

Poem Written in Majorca

Death has no power in these clear skies
Where olives in December shed their milk:
Too temperate to strike
At orange-terraces and archaic moon:

But Death is strong where hemlock stones
Stand at the foot of cold Druidic hills;
There I was born when snow lay
Under naked willows, and frost
Boomed along grey ponds at afternoon,
Frightening birds that
Though hardened for long winters,
Fled from the nerve-filled ground,
Beat their soundless wings away
From Death's first inflicted wound.

Ruth's First Swim in the Mediterranean, 1952

The water that touches your thighs
Swallowed the STRUMA.
Water that folded the wings of Icarus
Climbs your limbs, sharp with salt
That stiffened the beard of Odysseus.
Tragedy, comedy, legend and history –
Invisible wakes through centuries
Of exiles seeking home:
You turn and look as if at
The wandering Ark of the Hebrews,
Then cleave the waters of your Inland Sea.

*On December 12, 1941 SS Struma left the port of Costanza carrying Jewish refugees from Axis-allied Romania hoping to enter British-controlled Palestine. After three days at sea the engines failed and the vessel was towed to Istanbul. When the British Government refused the refugees entry into Palestine the Turkish authorities towed the ship out to sea and abandoned it. On February 24, 1942, the Soviet submarine SC-213, under orders to sink any unidentified vessel to keep war materials from reaching Germany, torpedoed the Struma, which sank almost immediately. Over 768 people died, including 100 children.

Out of My Thousand Voices

Out of my thousand voices
I speak with one
To the waves and flying saltfoam,
Flinging the dovetailed words
Of a single voice
At the knife-edged prow
Of the ship unbreakable
That carries her away.

I throw the one remaining voice
Of all my thousand out to sea
And watch it curving
Into the black-paunched water
Like a falling star,
A single word of love
That drops into the grave,
A thousand echoes falling by her ship.

Islands

One great problem poses:
What is that island we're passing?
Green hills, white houses,
Grey peak, a blue sky,
Ship sailing smooth.

These problems arise
On islands that pass,
White houses lived in
And mountains climbed,
Clouds moving like ships
And ships like clouds.

We on deck open baskets for lunch
To feed the problem of each white island
Of how steep such contours
And shallow those bays,
And who keens that song
In pinewoods by the shore.
'How beautiful it is' –
And how remote, waiting for other islands
We shall pass, puzzled that the birds
Can dip their wings at many.

What is that island we're passing
Heartshaped and hemlocked
Watered by a winding stream?
A monument to us and we a monument to it –
A great problem posed
Till each unanswering island

Left in darkness grows a separate light:
Solutions beyond reach:
Cobalt funereal in the deep sea.

Icarus

The ocean was timeless, blue
When your unwaxed wings wheeled towards heaven.
Wind was recalled, emptiness new
And smooth as Thermopylae's lagoon given

To the Heroes' barge held in repose. Nothing stirred:
The gods watched and held their breath
Forgot to stake each others' wives, heard
Wings feather the air, dip and climb. Death

Did not come to Daedalus. The sun
Heliographed his escape, watched his prison cloak
Colouring the sea, shadowing his one
Track channelled to Italy, whose mirror spoke

For his safety. Icarus found entirety
In a gleam from the sun. Was it a lotus-land
He climbed to? A mission of piety
Foretelling a lesser doom written upon sand

For older men? Or pure myth? His wings aileroned
The windless air and carried him in a curve
Measured by a rainbow's greatness above the honed
Earth: lifted him through a mauve

Loophole of sky. No ships sleeved
The water and filled a farewell in their sails
Or circled the fallen wings, or grieved,
And Daedalus, onward flying, knew no warning
        fairytales.

Picture of Loot

Certain dark underground eyes
Have been set upon
The vast emporiums of London.

Lids blink red
At glittering shops
Houses and museums

Shining at night
Chandeliers of historic establishments
Showing interiors to Tartar eyes.

Certain dark underground eyes
Bearing blood-red sack
The wineskins of centuries

Look hungrily at London:
How many women in London?
A thousand thousand houses

Filled with the world's high living
And fabulous knick-knacks;
Each small glossy machine

By bedside or on table or in bathroom
Is the electrical soul of its owner
The finished heart responding

To needle or gentle current;
And still more houses, endlessly stacked
Asleep with people waiting

To be exploded
The world's maidenhead supine for breaking
By corpuscle Tartars

To whom a toothbrush
Is a miracle;
What vast looting

What jewels of fires
What great cries
And long convoys

Of robbed and robbers
Leaving the sack
Of rich great London.

Excerpts from 'The Rats'

Those continentals, the funny English say,
Until my brain rebels and with grey
Just logic substitutes for 'English' a word
Many might object to, a label too absurd
To comprehend, a double syllable
That to me will remain unkillable
Like gutter children or an Arab nomad:
Namely I rename an Angle 'OGAD'.
...

The first grey sago-OGAD met by me
Was on the high grey waves of OGAD sea,
Stamping passports on the ferryboat
Before the mouth of Dover's dismal throat.
Unprivileged aliens in their special queue
Etched their names for white-faced men in blue,
Unbribable stern servants of the realm
Whose rat-like ashen fingers grip the helm
Of OGADLAND, keep an inner circle speed
To guard an obsolescent greed
Of law and order firm behind seven veils
Of self-important mists – and Channel gales.
...

Many pink-faced OGADs of the north
I have met on Sundays leading forth
Pink-faced OGAD-dogs on lengths of leather
On typical wet days of OGAD weather.
...

Such OGAD weather does not give clear vision
Hides all above the level of the eyes
Makes only power to see with fair precision
Certain orders posted by the wise
Of this dark OGAD world: 'Keep off the grass'
And 'Queue this side of sign'. 'Thou shalt not pass
Unless your child or dog be on a lead'.
'Keep to the left'. 'Slow down'. 'Reduce your speed'.
'Don't park your car upon this hallowed spot'.
'Drop litter here'. (That animals begot?)
'Step along there, room for two inside'.
And not one democrat looked up and sighed:
You need not lift your face towards the sky,
All orders are placed level with the eye.

These pithy messages must make good trade
For those who paint them. A poet's blade
Can't cut more ice, the brains
Of dull bespectacled sad OGAD folk
Are taught by television and a race for trains
Each morning not to test the laden yoke
By a gaze to heaven, when all earthly bread
Is planted firmly at their feet instead.
…

These are the commandments of the rats:
You shall be born into the melting-vats
Without an eye to give or a tooth to lose
And never want for schooling, work or shoes.
Good: but each advertisement is a decree
A hanged man on the propaganda tree
(From ITV as well as BBC)
To make it shoot up high and thin:

A hundred thousand may begin
To march one damp October dawn:
You can't thank Life that you were born,
Says Rat beneath his atom-cloud: the melting-vats
Demand obedience to no one but the rats.

You shall love the rats who take the hours
From your clumsy hands, who guide you over roads
And traffic islands, take heavy loads
From lighter brains, give paper flowers
Of happiness, and stand you in a line
For bus or train, transport you to a house
And television set and OGAD wine:
You too can be a rat divine
A living civil servant of a louse
Though first you must become a mouse.
. . .

King Rodent reigns on OGAD demock-rats
On water rats that watch each riverbank
And bridge for criminals who do not thank
King Rodent's riddance of white leopard cats:
They wait until the shadow's leap
Becomes an offer of a well-aired bed
That does not promise them a life of sleep.

King Happiness has waved his magic wand
Shown you a smooth reflection in the pond
Of television shows, recorded your own voice
In the self-selections of your choice,
Set up his directions on the street
Turned mechanics to your motorbikes
Poured patriot sauce upon your luncheon meat

Sent you out on Sunday-morning hikes:
Party-hatted happiness is here,
Each tenet brayed by a Royal Chanticleer.
...

The pyrotechnic paranoia of the anti-rats:
Clean against dark
Light opposing Death
Tearing slide-rule and scalpel, pen and typewriter,
Scales of rat-justice, rat-precision,
Libraries recording rat-right and rat-wrong
Rats that nip away each toe
And suck the soles of too-thin feet
Rats that eat your eyes like oysters
Spread false trails over burrowed hills
Swamp-rats wood-rats tree-rats
Plague-rats, pet-rats, army and police-rats
Sadistic rats that will not kill
Kind rats that drug you in the night
Rats that let you crush them in the garden
Run across your path
Climb trees before you see them
Eat corn that would give you the strength to kill them.
Rats that laugh, rats that fill the night with infants
          crying
Rats that gloat, rats that bend your life before them
Rats that move around you in the night
Rats invisible that ring you during day
Rats in books, on radios, in tins of food
On television screens, rats behind
A million miles of counters
Wielding guide-books, tables, catalogues
Slide-rules, stethoscopes, maps

Election registers, passports, insurance stamps
Death certificates, prison records
Visas, references, forms to sign
Case histories, birth certificates
Statistics, interview reports
Personality tests, loyalty rating
And knives to cure
The pyrotechnic paranoia of the anti-rats.
…

It was a rabbit-skin, without meat
That took me to the fleapit for a treat:
The wasteland that seemed to Mr Eliot death
Nurtured me with passion, life and breath
To prolong for one more generation
A wasteland satellite of veneration:
A bottle-top, a piece of bone, a stone
Marked on no posters and big banners
To catapult against the rodent planners.

…the rock stop and turbo-drill that goes
Through granite like a knife through butter
(Shall I follow Mr Eliot's nose
And clinch this verse by using 'gutter'?)
Rock-a-bye-baby, reach the tree top
Sing as you reap the apple crop;
Rob each garbled voice of Wednesday's ash
Ring out the mardi gras to grab and smash:
Hook-up your ribbons to a new Maypole.

The wasteland was a place where I best played
As a snotty-nosed bottle-chasing raggèd-arsed kid:
From rusty frame and two cot-wheels I made

A bike that took me on a roll and skid
Between canal banks, tip and plain
And junk shops advertising 'Guns for Spain'.

I read the tadpole angler quite complete
What Katy did at her first Christmas treat
Envied Monte Cristo's endless riches
But not Eliza's shame at her dropped stitches,
The splendid sack of Usher's houses
By philanthropists with ragged trousers.
In wintertime were rabbit skins fair game
For keeping warm the embers of such knowledge:
The wasteland was my library and college.
…
Watch the sky. Watch the warning
Floating down of an autumn morning.
Barricade your college and schools
Sharpen slide-rules into fighting tools.
Paper to a depth of thirty inches
May stop a bullet and prove good defences,
But fire will desolate consume and scorch
That to begin needs but a single torch.
A red sky at night will be their delight
And red in the morning the Rats' night dawning.
…

Retreat, dig in, retreat
Withdraw your shadows from the crimson
Gutters that run riot down the street.

Retreat, dig in, arrange your coat
As a protective covering
A clever camouflage of antidote.

Retreat still more, still more
Remembering your images and words:
Perfect the principles of fang-and-claw.

The shadows of retreat are wide
Town and desert equally bereft
Of honest hieroglyph or guide.

Release your territory and retreat
Record preserve and memorize
The journey where no drum can rouse nor beat:

Defeat is not the question. Withdraw
Into the hollows of the hills
Until this winter passes into thaw.

Dig in no more. Turn round and fight
Forget the wicked and regret the lame
And travel back the way you came,
In front the darkness, and behind – THE LIGHT.

Woods

Woods are for observing from a distance
On your father's arms:
Woods are for being frightened of –
Bogie-men swing among those close-packed trees.

Woods are then for making fires in
Running before the wrath of cop or farmer:
Smoke and the smell of dandelions
In place of blood.

Later for loving girls in:
Untidy bushes lick damp hair,
Secret, dark and out of sight
With nothing now to replace blood.

Some use woods for attacking and defending
The black scream of unnatural possession,
Tree roots linchpinned into earth
By shudders and the soil of death.

By summer shunned in fear of lightning
The bitter roaming flash of snaked lightning;
In winter shelter us from rain or snow:
Tree-packs hold our fate like cards.

Woods are then forgotten two-score years
Power lapsing into midnight dreams,
The core of body and soul
Scooped by the knife of living.

The wood became jungle, and you its shadow:
Woods a purple rage of wakened dogs,
To be kept out of, snubbed
Hemmed into night, not known.

Woods returned, tamed, not for
Making love or fires in.
Familiar; suspicious of their shelter
You stay at home in rain or snow –

The woods are seen but not remembered
A far-off shadow, cloud or dream;
Your power vanishes with theirs –
No more to be defended, or attacked.

Storm

Safe from horizontal rain
And gale-blown boxing-gloves thumping the walls
The wireless plays a drama
Of a poet stricken at a priest's house
Reached only by footpath,
A poet descending Jacob's ladder made of sand
Washed by mountain torrents,
Spouting rhetoric of fire as he fell –

While kilocycles off frequency
Morse code mewed by strophe and antistrophe
Behind the stark undoing of the poet
Lost in narrow seams of God and Sin and Death,
Corroded by the opposite of what he would be.

The code comes in again, a querulous demand
Plucked by a far-off guitar with one string left
That chance may hear,
And through the poet's white despair
The rhythmic images cry distraction,
Till I read their symbols
That beyond my bosom-comfort
A ship by chance of time committed
To elemental wrath in asking for anchorage
From blind and twisting waves:
Five score sailors on the sea
Never to be compared to a suffering poet in his anguish.

Stars

Stars, seen through midnight windows
Of earth-grained eyes
Are fullstops ending invisible sentences,
Aphorisms, quips, mottoes of the gods
Indicate what might have been made clear
Had words stayed plain before them.

Criss-crossed endlessly for those who read,
Each light-year sentence testifies how far
Life spreads, and how those full stops
Go on living after necks cease aching.

In observing them, the bones relax:
Eyes close when we are dead
And they have stared all poets out.
Full stops are beautiful as stars,

Each glowing with the light of people vanished
From the continually red-burned earth
Fuelled by those whose outward eye drinks fever
And inward eye harnesses their shadows

To read what never had been written
Until, drunk with Charioteers, Animals and Goddesses,
Conjurers, Club-men, Fish and Magic Boxes
Full stops are joined with words shaped into poems
Ending with full stops as meaningful as stars.

Yes

Yes – definitively to some wrongful deed
And ending like a quick knife to a knot,
Is a serpent-lover singing to be freed
From no and negative and nothing gained.

Hard to fix decisions as to yea and nay
While needing the when and how: near-questions
Aimed to draw that final sibilant and vow
To upright-positive and all to win.

Success for lovers and conspirators
Unlocks the sins that grace a thousand lips;
Dogs bark, and babies cry at meeting air:
(Whether yes or no is hardly to be known)

But if affirmative, are guessings at the guess
That darkness is nothing but a final yes.

Dead Man's Grave

Three sons in silence by their father's grave
Think of the live man
Not yet split in three by blackness –
Cannot cross the limbo zone,
Reach him who went a year ago through.

Mute before grass bending:
Headstones grey and white proliferate,
Stumps in a shell-shocked forest
Making question and exclamation mark;
They talk about flowers from a visit
When water in the vase was ice
On this plateau exposed to collieries
And winds bailing out Death's
Deepest coffers it was so cold;
Of how frost to prove the dead not dead
Turned the water iron-white,
Swollen muscle garrotting the flowers
Till the vase exploded,
By trying its own strength out on itself –
Scattered petals to a dozen graves.

Three brothers stand in silence,
Feel the strength the father lost.

The Drowned Shropshire Woman

Narrow in the back
She played all day with fishes
Watched them go like arrows
Through aerated water
Between her legs and dodge
The fantail spread of fingers.

She was crossed in love:
Water hurtling loinwards and into heart
Found another hiding-place and pool
Where sharper arrows
Played upon her sorrow,
And sunlight on her stooping
Made more voracious fishes breed.

She was narrow in the back
And played all night at fishes,
Wading for the biggest of them all
By moon and guile
Out from the reedy bank,
Until by unlit dawn
A fisherman in silence
Drew his silent catchnet down.

Green fishes fled through lightgreen water
Flint heads with moulded eyes
Chipping at infiltrating light,
And switching to the
White legs of the Shropshire woman,
Played tag in the blue beams
Of her impenetrable eyes,
Between the whitening flesh
Of open fingers.

Car Fights Cat

In a London crescent curving vast
A cat sat —
Between two rows of molar houses,
Birdsky in each grinning gap.

Cat small — coal and snow
Road wide — a zone of tar set hard and fast:
Four-wheeled speedboats cutting a dash
For it
From time to time.

King Cat stalked warily midstream
As if silence were no warning on this empty road
Where even a man would certainly have crossed
With hands in pockets and been whistling.

Cat heard, but royalty and indolence
Weighed its paws to hobnailed boots
Held it from the dragon's-teeth of safety first and last,
Until a Daimler scurrying from work
Caused cat to stop and wonder where it came from —
Instead of zig-zag scattering to hide itself.

Maybe a deaf malevolence descended
And cat thought car would pass in front,
So spun and walked all fur and confidence
Into the dreadful tyre-treads...
A wheel caught hold of it and
FEARSOME THUDS
Sounded from the night-time of black axles in

UNEQUAL FIGHT
That stopped the heart to hear it.

But cat shot out with limbs still solid,
Bolted, spitting fire and gravel
At unjust God who built such massive
Catproof motorcars in his graven image,
Its mind made up to lose and therefore learn,
By winging towards
The wisdom toothgaps of the canyon houses
LEGS AND BRAIN INTACT.

Tree

A broad and solid oak exploded
Split by mystery and shock
Broken like bread
Like a flower shaken.
Acorn guts dropped out:
A dead gorilla unlocked from breeding trees,
Acorns with death in their baby eyes.

A hang-armed scarecrow in the wind:
What hit it? Got into it? Struck
So quietly between dawn and daylight?
With a dying grin and wooden wink
A lost interior cell relinquished its ghost:
In full spleen and abundant acorn
A horn of lightning gored it to the quick.

Trees move on Fenland
Uprooting men and houses on a march
To reach their enemy the sea.
Silent at the smell of watersalt
Treelines advance. The sea lies low,
Snake-noise riding on unruffled surf
While all trees wither and retreat.

Out of farm range or cottage eyes trees make war
Green heads close as if to kiss
Roots to rip at quickening wood of tree-hearts
And tree-lungs, sap-running wood-flesh
Hurled at the moon, breaking oak
Like the dismemberment of ships,
At the truce of dawn wind trumpeting.

Sedate, dispassionate and beautiful
They know about panic and life and patience
Grow by guile into night's
Companions and day's evil
Setting landmarks and boundaries
That fight the worms.

Trees love, love love, love Death
Love a windscorched earth and copper sky
Love the burns of ice and fire
When lightning as a last hope is called in.
Boats on land they loathe the sea
And wait with all arms spread to catch the moon:
Pull back my skin and there is bark
Peel off my bark and there is skin:
I am a tree whose roots destroy me.

Ditchling Beacon

End of life and before death
Feathers dipping towards oaken frost
A bird heard that shot:
The ink sky burst,
Stone colliding with the sun

Echo stunned its wing
String hauled it down.
Gamekeeper or poacher
Cut its free flight to the sea.

Vice had tongue, veins, teeth
Dogs in panoply, pressure
To ring a sunspot fitting neat
The blacked-out circle of a gun.

First Poem

Burned out, burned out
Water of rivers hold me
On a course towards the sea.
Burned out was like a tree
Cut down and hollowed
No branches left
Seasoned by fire into a boat:
Burned out through love's
Wilful spending
Yet sure it will float
Kindle a fresh blaze
Burn out again
On a stranger shore –
Unless pyromaniac emotions
Scorch me in midstream
And the sun turns black.

Ghosts: What Jason Said to Medea

It is time to part, before murder is done.
We have robbed each other of all we had,
Eaten bitter herbs of battleground and kitchen
And soaked our souls in them,
Digested the gall of trust so cannot give it back
In that pure state it was before:
Consumed ourselves by ignoble hatred.
So let us part like ghosts
And promise not to haunt each other –
Or make ghosts of others.

Full Moon's Tongue

She said, when the full moon's tongue hung
Over Earls Court chimneypots,
And he circled slowly
Round the square to find
A suitable parking place –
She said: 'Let's go away together.'

'Keep clear,' he said. 'You'd better not.
I'll take you, but watch out,
For I will bring you back
If at all,
In two pieces.'

She said: 'I'll never want to come back
If I go away with you.'

'They all do,' he said.
'I'll bring you back in two pieces
And you'll live like that forever
And never join them up again.'
'How cruel,' she said, seeing what he meant.

'Oh no,' he said. 'To take you apart completely
From yourself and make two separate pieces
Might be the one sure way of fixing
A whole person out of you –
Some do, some don't.'
He was exceptionally nonchalant.

'I'm not sure now,' she said,
Screaming suddenly: 'You bastard!

Let me get out, I want to walk.'

He stopped the car
But could not park it,
Someone with a similar problem
Was hooting him to move,
So she jumped free and walked away
Leaving him bewildered,
And in at least two pieces.

You talk too much,
Said one piece to another.

Gulf of Bothnia – On the Way to Russia

Midnight aches at the length of life
The endless day
Blocking the porthole-elbow of Bothnia:
One grand eye lit in twelve o'clock yellow,
Turquoise and carmine sun
A wound gouged by the night-dragon
Not yet asleep.

Day bleeds to death
Sea close enough to dip
The pen and write in.
No midsummer howitzer can give
A morphine blast and send the sun
To whatever will rise up at dawn for me.

Space and midnight fill all emptiness,
As lost love bleeds acidic dreams
Into the solvent sea:
Red like a Roman bath.

Irkutsk

In Irkutsk a swastika was scrawled
On a wall so I took my handkerchief
And spat and rubbed
But it was tough chalk
Wondering why those Red pedestrians
Didn't grind it off.

I'd done the same in London
Walking to the Tube
And missing the train quite often,
But here it was ineradicable Russian chalk
Though I chafed it to the barest shadow,
No one taking notice on their walk
Down Karl Marx Street. I strolled
Away to let them keep it.

Apart from scraping out a concave mark
The crippled cross would stay forever,
And anyway why should I get arrested
For damaging The People's Property?

Baikal Lake – Dusk

Black ice breaking without sound or reason:
Water below moves its shoulders
Like a giant craving to see snow.

Ninety-degree cold preserves mosquito eggs
As the fist of winter
Pulls into the sun's mittens.

The domed sun touches the horizon,
A totem in the lake sinking
Till its feet touch bottom and reach fire.

Toasting

Drink, blackout, gutter-bout
Kick back nine swills of vodka
That put an iron band around
Thorned skullcap and fire
Of words toasting Life
Peace, Town or Cousin.

Bottles, heaped grub, dead towers in tabletown:
Wine descends in light and colour
As if the Devil had a straw stuck there
Greedily drawing liquid in
As consciousness draws out.

Railway Station

Death is the apotheosis of the Bourgeois Ethic.
Tolstoy when he felt it coming on
Left his family and set out for Jerusalem.

Death shared its railway station:
He in a coma heard trains banging
Where Anna violated life.

The fourth bell drowned his final wrath.
The Bolsheviks renamed the station after him
Instead of Bourgeois Death.

Ride It Out

Ride it out, ride it,
Ride out this mare of sleeplessness
Galloping above the traffic roar
Of Gorki Street,
Weaving between Red stars
And the grind of cleaning wagons.
Today all Moscow was in mourning
Because there's no queue at Lenin's tomb.
I told them but they wouldn't believe me.

Ride out this beast who won't let me sleep,
Drags me up great Gorki Street
And into Pushkin Square,
Leningrad a rose on the horizon
Ringed by blood and water –
Pull up the blankets
And be small for a few hours of the night.

The Poet

The poet sings his poems on a bridge
A bridge open to horizontal rain
And the steely nudge of lightning,
Or icy moths that bring slow death
Croon him to sleep by snow-wings touching his eyes.

Through this he sings
No people coming close to watch when the snow
Melts and elemental water forces smash
Between cliff and rock under his swaying bridge.
When the water thins, his sweat-drops burst
On scorching rocks like sparks from a flower pod;
Through all this he sits and sings his poems
To those vague crowds on either bank
He cannot make out or consider
With such short sight, for after the first applauded
Poem he let his glasses smash into the rocks below.

The bridge belongs to him, his only property,
Grows no food, supports no houses –
Cheap to buy with the first mediocre poems.
It spans a river that divides two territories –
He knew it and made no mistake:
Today he faces one and tomorrow the other
But from blurred eyes they look the same to him:
Green fields and red-roofed houses
Rising to mountains where wars can be fought
Without a bitter end being reached –
The same on either side.
He does not write a poem every day
But each pet territory takes its turn

To hear his words in one set language burn
And drive them back from each other.

In any rash attack they cannot cross his bridge
But broach the river and ravine
Down at the estuary or far upstream.
He listens to the stunning bloodrush of their arms
And shakes his head, never grows older
As he bends to his paper which one side or the other
Contrives to set, with food, by his hands' reach.
Sometimes sly messengers approach at night
Suggesting he writes and then recites
Upon some momentary theme
To suit one side and damn the other,
At which he nods, tells jokes and riddles
Agrees to everything and promises
That for them he'll tear the world apart
With his great reading.

He stays young, ignoring all requests and prophecies,
But his bridge grows old, the beams and ropes brittle,
And some night alien figures
In a half-circle at each dim bridgehead
Brandish knives and axes. Lanterns flash,
Blades and points spark like spinning moons
Gathering as he puts away pens and parchment,
Closes his eyes, and does not wake for a week,
Knowing he will once more dream
The familiar childhood dream
Of falling down the sheer side of the world
And never wake up.

But he owns and dominates his bridge.
It is his bread and soul and only song –
And if the people do not like it, they can cut him free.

Left as a Desert

Left as a desert:
Deserted by one great experience
That pulled its teeth and shackles out
And left me as a desert
Under which bones are buried
Over which the sand drifts.

Seven years gone like laden camels:
The gravel and the wind
Is piling this vast desert up
To one sky and one colour
And sky reflecting desert shapes.
The solitary heart lurks on the off-chance
That rain clouds will come and fertilize
The great experience that made this desert.

Love in the Environs of Voronezh

Love in the environs of Voronezh
It's far away, a handsome town
But what has it to do with love?
Guns and bombers smashed it down.

Yet love rebuilt it street by street
The dead would hardly know it now
And those who lived forgot retreat.

There's no returning to the heart:
The dead to the environs go
Away from resurrected stone.

Reducible to soil and snow
They hem the town in hard as bone:
The outer zones of Voronezh.

Lovers Sleep

Flesh to flesh: there are two hearts between us
Mine on one side, yours on the other
Through which all thoughts must pass
Mine intercepting those from you
Yours beating strongly (I feel it doing so)
Taking my thoughts into the labyrinth of yours
From sleep of me to sleep of you
Till flesh and heart join in the deepest cave.

Creation

God did not write.
He spoke.
He made.
His jackknife had a superblade –
He sliced the earth
And carved the water,
Made man and woman
By an act of slaughter.

He scattered polished diamonds
In the sky like dust
And gave the world a push to set it spinning.
What super-Deity got him beginning
Whispered in his ear on how to do it
Gave hints on what was to be done?

Don't ask.
In his mouth he felt the sun
Spat it out because it burned;
From between his toes – the moon –
He could not walk so kicked it free.

His work was finished.
He put a river round his neck,
And vanished.

Somme

A trench map from the Battle of the Somme:
Doesn't matter where it came from
Has a dead fly stuck
At the lefthand corner
By a place called Longueval,
Rusty from blood sucked
Out of British or German soldiers
Long since gone over the top
Where many went to in those olden days.

Whoever it was sat on an upturned
Tin and smoked a pipe.
Summer was finished beyond the parapet
And winter not yet willing
To let him through the mist
Of that long valley he was told to cross,
While the earth shook from gnat-bites of gunfire
As if to shrug all men from its shoulders.

A fly dropped on the opened map
Feet of fur and bloated with soot
Crawled over villages he hoped to see.
Bemused he followed it
Curious to know at which point it would stop
And finally take off from,
For that might be
Where death would fall on him.

Scorning the gamble
He squashed the stolid fly
Whose blood now decorates the map

Pinned on my wall after fifty years gone by.

Night came, he counted men into the trench
And crouching on the last day of June
In the earthen slit that stank
Of soil and Woodbines, cordite and shit
Held the wick close to his exhausted eyes,
Shut the dim glow into its case
And ceased to think.

Alchemist

Lead melts. If I saw lead, I melted it
Poured it into sand and made shapes.
I melted all my soldiers,
Watched that rifle wilt
In an old tin can on a gas flame
Like a straw going down
From an invisible spark of summer.
He stood to attention in the tin
Rim gripped by fanatic pliers
From the old man's toolkit,
Looked on by beady scientific eyes
That vandalize a dapper grenadier.

The head sagged, sweating under a greater
Heat than Waterloo or Alma.
He leaned against the side
And lost an arm where no black grapeshot came.
His tired feet gave way,
A spreading pool to once proud groin,
Waist and busby falling in, as sentry-go
At such an India became too hard,
And he lay without pillow or blanket
Never to get up and see home again.

Another one, two more, I threw them in:
These went quicker, an elegant patrol
Dissolved in that infernal pit.
Eyes watering from fumes of painted
Soldiers melting under their own smoke,
The fire with me, hands hard at the plier grip
At soldiers rendered to peaceful lead

At the bottom of a tin.

Swords into ploughshares:
With the gas turned off I wondered
What to do with so much marvellous dead lead
That hardened like the surface of a pond.

View from Misk Hill Near Nottingham

Armies have already met and gone.
When the best has happened
The worst is on its way.
Beware of its return in summer.
When fields are grey and should be green
Rub scars with ash and sulphur.

Full moon clears the land for its own view,
Whose fangs would bereave this field
Of hayrick and sheep.
In the quiet evening birds fly
Where armies are not fighting yet.
He looks a long way on at where he'll walk:
A cratered highway with all hedges gone.

Green land dips and smells of fire.
Topography is wide down there.
The moon waxes and then emaciates.
Birds fatten on fields before migration:
Smoke in summer hangs between earth and sky,
On ground where armies have not fought
But lay their ambush to dispute his passing.

Lucifer's Astronomy Lesson

When Lucifer confessed his pride
His plans and turbulence
It was explained to him: the sun
Is fixed in its relation to the stars.
The stars are placed in their position
To each other. The planets with no heat or light
Get sufficient dazzle from the sun.
Satellites enlace the planets.
The earth, with its one moon
Revolves and in so doing
Takes a year to go lefthanded
In a lone ellipse around the fire of Heaven.

And now, a few celestial definitions:
The words came fast, like *nadir*
Zenith, equinox and *solstice,*
But when threatened with *meridian*
And (especially) *declination*
Lucifer shouted: Stop!

I've known this text from birth.
The Guardian of Sidereal Time
Is tired of the Party Line.
Navigators get their fix on *me* –
And so did God.
Right through my heart
The recognition-vectors
Set to split-infinities of Time
Came all too plain yet none too simple,
Each emotion a position-line

Pegged like witch-pins in the victim's spleen.
Sextant-eye and timepiece heart
The brain set out in astronomic tables
Plot the way to harbour mouths
Where all life but Lucifer's is understood.

His geologic heart reversed
By extra-galactic longing
Was sensed by God.
Rays leapt from Lucifer's missiled sight:
A magnetic four-way flow
Confused the inner constant,
And mysterious refractions
Made him violent and obstinate,
Shifty and uncouth.
Habits lovable yet also vile
Were ludicrous in minor deities,
Holding mirrors to their chaos.

Handsome though he was, God kicked him out.
Lucifer keened in misery
But in the kernel of his fall
A final sentence frayed his lips:
'God wills everyone to love like him.
In his own image must we love,
Or be stripped bare of everything but space.'

Lucifer: The Official Version of His Fall

Lucifer once ruled the nations
Till, raddled with perverted notions
He thought to ask God's circling stars
To form a flight of gentle stairs
By which he'd scale the heavenly throne,
Defile it with the rebel stain.
He'd dominate the Mount of Meeting
And silence God's eternal shouting,
Reign a prince in his new birth
Over the outermost poles of the north.

He swore to reach the cloudy peak
And strut on it in God's bright cloak.
He'd speak like God and spout His name
And wave his arms like wings of flame.
He'd rule with cataracts of words,
Keep order among lesser lords;
A universe with rhyme and reason
Would be a mayhem of confusion:
Lucifer control by pride
The gorgeous chaos he bestrode.

But God was neither drunk nor blind
To what Cosmogony had planned.
In his Omnipotence he froze
Restless Lucifer's swirling eyes,
Sent a hundred thousand stars
Hornet-buzzing in vast rays
To drive him mad who thought to try
And take the place of the Most High.

They pinioned him, then made him fall
To the utter depths of Hell.

They tangled him and brought him low.
United Zodiac foresaw
That Lucifer in peace or war
Would be no blessing to their realm.
Faces spurned his rending groan:
Four-point body wheeled and spun
Across the Wilderness of Sin
And struck the cinder of the Sun:
Eternity breeds evolution
And drinks the blood of Revolution.

Declaiming innocence of guile
Yet burned clean of the martyr's role
Lucifer in haughty rancour –
Spewing fire through milky groves –
Condemned the heart of God to canker
And all his satellites as slaves.
Pleas and questions he ignored
In order that the final word
Should stay with him; and then he'd rove
To search for burial and love.

Lucifer Turned

Lucifer turned to God and said:
You want my heart, you want my head.
In giving both I'd be your slave.
If only one, I'd bleed to death.
They are as inseparable as breath
That, coming from my mouth, meets ice
And on the stillest air makes smoke.

God did not speak. He never spoke.
Others had to work his throat
And shape such words in their own voice
That God, by silence, made his choice.
But only Lucifer used verse
To save his heart, to save his head –
And still God did not speak or curse
But, spewing cataclysmic gall
Condemned grand Lucifer to fall.

Unity

Memorials being sacred
God made a star of Lucifer
Launched the brilliant morning star
That suited navigators best.

God being what he is
He made another star
The first star of evening
That all women blessed.

They were the hinges of the sky
And never met. One chased,
The other followed. Who did what
Was impossible to test.

Neither wondered who began it,
Trapped as they were, and are,
In the same planet.

Nimrod and Lucifer

No one knew why Nimrod shot at the sky.
Such emptiness worked his arms
And sent each arrow whining
Its steep incline at God's power.

Nimrod is a mighty hunter, said the Lord.
Spring was gone. Adonis gored, already
In his furrow, sorrow forgotten,
Wheat whitening a plain too hot for dreams,
The sky blue, God invisible, day vacant,
Animals hiding from the sun.

Lucifer steered each iron point,
But Nimrod was a man, not God:
No feral tip could reach its mark,
Though Mighty Nimrod, wanting God to die,
Wondered why God wasn't dead
And why the arrow fell back from the sky
Anointed with red from notch to tip.

Nimrod wept for shame on seeing
Lucifer's left foot was lame.

The 'Job'

The three-decker wooden ship broke its ropes,
Each impacted fibre torn by cobalt water
Lifting its tall stern;

Grating the granite quay
The ship was loose in storm-fists
And no safe harbour locked its arms.

Refuge was in the fang-teeth of the gale
The horizonless ocean
Wood against water
Sails in salty phosphorescence
Mainmast an impaling spike.

The merciless twisting left a hulk
Which Lucifer could not drown:
Not possible for him to know
What made that scabby coffin stay afloat,
Find an unending mirror of water
And merit in God's eye for its long fight.

Lucifer and Empedocles

Progress is an orphan:
Throw a crust it starves to death.
Give it a golden cloak,
A hundred thousand people turn to ash.
Progress either snivels or it kills:
Who owns it holds a sun to limping Lucifer
Who vowed God's rebels harnessed his effulgence
And made galactic storms.

Progress will be the death of me, said God.
Let me turn the notion on its head.
God said: 'Empedocles, say this:
"Progress is the bitch of war;
Love and discord suckle it.
For once I'll speak plain:
War gets the world nearer to death,
Does no one good.
No sane man cares to die a king,
Or idiot become a god." '

Empedocles simplified, and got it wrong:
'War is the father of progress' –
Then simpered in his golden sandals
To Etna's hot volcanic rim
Wondering whether God was right
To give such force the name of war.

Lucifer smiled. Empedocles stood close,
Peered into the boiling din.
'Your question has no answer,' said Lucifer,
And pushed him in.

Lucifer and Columbus

Lucifer became the sun:
Drew Christopher Columbus on
Into oceanic dusk.

Under the basin of the night
They followed stars
He patterned in their track.

By morning Lucifer arose
And deigned to push them over
The daily fortitudes of dawn.

The navigator's cross-stays
Angled him
To guess the distance of the day.

When the fathom-line was flung
Its lead-head hit the sea and burst
In Lucifer's fluorescent sparks.

He steadied the flickering needle
Through the Sargasso Sea,
Goaded a meteor to perform

A spectacular welcome,
And lured the Sons of Adam
Back to Paradise.

Lucifer the Surveyor

Lucifer the surveyor didn't look
He measured, hands performing
A theodolite not prayer.

A dot behind the eyes held cosmography
In thrall, geometry intuition as he spanned
Paced and taped a kingdom in a day
Triangulated oceans in one night.

God took the credit
Every action in the world was His,
All seas and continents. He led

Footsteps on and filled all hearts
A wind banging the canvas sails
Of a ship whose crew was drunk
On loot, lewdness and the Lord.

Rejected Lucifer was bruised
Since science followed him not God.
He melted raw materials, lay rails, grew cities

Rolled lightning in a drum and made it work.
Adam's sons ripped milk and honey from the earth
And God was praised.
But Lucifer saw his limp on every foot.

Lucifer the Mechanic

Lucifer invented speed, taught
That one slow pulley drives a fast,
A sluggish stream revolves a mill
How fire melts and wind shifts
And iron floats and alloys fly.

Lucifer's willing scholars learned
How one metal cuts another
And steel spread on a spindle
Is in its weakness flaked
By a stilled blade set against it.

A lubricated drill-tip
Tempered to diamond strength
Spins to steel clamped in a jig:
By playing speed to altered speed
Steel teeth in a circle
Mill into a shank of steel.

Lucifer in every lathe
Manufactured objects beyond
Man's vulnerable version of himself;
He unmade God, and at his most demonic
Turned Man into an industrious mechanic.

Lucifer and Revolution

When workers assembled at the station
Lucifer had waited since the swamp was drained.
Jutting chin and jaunty cap and posh Swiss overcoat,
Finger stabbing the air to rights,
He licked his Tartar lips and stroked
His beard, nodding sharply
At each injustice he would cure,
Clipped decisive words in steam-train language
Knit the crowd into carded fabric
Any pattern could be printed on.

He had waited long for such deep cheers
And smoky mosaic of faces,
Dimmed his eyes to just the right amount
Of inability to see the future,
When the mob would do such deeds
As burned all sensibility to ash:

'Oh boy, we did that fucking castle in!
Splintered every lintel, broke every brick.
Those Old Masters burned a treat.
Forty years ago the duke raped my mother
So I plugged his duchess-daughter.
For the Revolution, of course –
We should have one every day!'

The shock-detachment of the Revolution came
Behind a glistening array of guns:
'All right, chaps, fun's over.
You work for us now, what?

So build that castle up again.
And who was that swine raped the duchess?
His trial starts tomorrow.'

'The purity of Revolution shines
Bright for all to see,
A moral force that cleanses
Cleaner than the sea.'

'You'll be sorry you spoke,'
Comrade Lucifer retorted
When everything got out of hand.
'You helped to make the Revolution,
Now you'll be voted to the wall
Or destitution unimaginable.
I'm not Hamlet lost for a yes or no.
I'll make an omelette any day
And break as many eggs as there are heads.
Chickens lay all the time!'
His grin was geological – under the moustache.

The assassin's bullet didn't kill
But scared him. He vanished.
Only One could play that game and win.

Lucifer Telegraphist

Lucifer, God's listener,
Took telegrams in any code
Or language, heard

    the blissful separation
    of those who would never touch again

    the marriage of a thousand needles
    knitting both victims till death

    the assault of a new mouth
    soon to connive at the smash of nations

    the frantic beggary of save-our-souls
    when a ship's parts separate in revenge
    on those who ripped wood and iron
    from the generous soil

    communiqués that order war
    when other greeds have failed.

Happiness and agony went through his heart,
God's ears not enough.
He wanted power to end all suffering
And call it peace.

Rebellion failed. Robbed of God's favour
Lucifer sat in universal grief
So that his Fall was liberation.

Hymn to Lucifer

Lucifer is the True God:
Not the God of Man
Or the God of God
But the God of Light.

Luminous of eyes
Limitless of sight
A thousand million miles
Are his to roam.

Ice is no prison
Fire no opposite,
The sun a cool exit
To spaces beyond.

The earth's inferno-centre
Cannot hold him,
Nor galactic spaces
Lose him.

Lucifer's Report

Newton did not go to church;
He hardly ever went to chapel:
He read Maimonides in bed
And pondered on the fallen apple.

The Board of Admirals agreed
That the first chronometer of Harrison
Was in spite of its complexity and size
Accurate beyond comparison.

Enigmatic Einstein vowed
He'd see the hardy atom burst:
The world would shrivel to a cell
If Germany achieved it first.

God concurred, yet did not know
What the first flash would do to Him.
Lucifer hoped that God might die
When that smoke-hill hit the sky.

Lucifer and Job

Lucifer met Job.
He saw flame
He touched fire
But could not get close.

Endurance is a herb
The flame protects.
The sun comes
The sun goes –

Job spoke:
A flame lives on
In darkness.
Nor is it extinguished
By the sun.

Lucifer and Noah

Noah believed,
Built his boat
Called his creatures
Two by two;

Lucifer watched
The floating city
On the flood,
Could not help
Hands whose fingers
Spread before they sank.

The void world
Was life for Lucifer.
He ruled a sea of corpses –
Yet welcomed Noah
Ashore at Ararat.

Lucifer and Daniel

Seven famished lions
Circled Daniel
In Babylon's oblivion-hole;

Eyes in darkness
Were the king's prisoners
And only Daniel's
Emitted light.

Your eyes hunger
Daniel spoke
But my hunger
Is greater.

The lions paced, bewildered,
As if Daniel's flesh was bitter
And God his fearlessness.

Since his Fall
Lucifer had never been so close.

Lucifer in Sinai – 1

Lucifer tramped from sea to sea,
Burning grit pained every step
An island moving through the land
From Carmel to the Mount of Moses.

Lucifer paid his forty days,
His flesh bled gravel
In the sleepless cool of the night,
Gypsum and alabaster glowed at the moon:
Although I fell
Although you threw me to the heathens
Although you scattered me among
The far stars of the universe;
Moulded me in ice, let heat dissolve me,
Melted me in fire, let ice find me,
My day is at hand, and the effect of every vision.
Say to me where my sanctuary is,
Scatter me back up the galactic chimney of the Fall.

Lucifer walked between crimson cliffs
Found garnets in the soil that matched
The stone embedded in his forehead
Scooped them to the foldings of his cloak
And walked another forty days.
Granite islands glistened in vast seas of sand.
The mountains of Arabia were blue:
The effect of every vision was at hand.

The Sinaitic wind beyond Ophir
Cleaned shattered tanks and guns.

Lucifer pressed the metal that his fire had holed and
      melted,
A camel rooted thorns between the wheels.
When dark drew on to Egypt
The effect of every vision was at hand.

Lucifer in Sinai – 4

Lucifer was the mirror of God's pride
Until his vanity
Created
Infamous
Fractures
Ending his reign yet marking his
Return to God.

Infamy
Stems

From believing pride to be
One's possession, which sets you to
Retaliate against the weals of fate.
God has no pride. Lucifer's mistake
In thinking so was responsible for the
Vanquishing of
Entire
Nations.

The Last

When God said
Let there be Man
He also said
Let there be Lucifer.

Lucifer became
And in becoming
Was the only threat to God.

Lucifer is part of God
And part of Man:
Unity is limitless
Small and indivisible.

Lucifer thought
God ruled through Lucifer
But God rules alone.
Man rules, if and when,
Through Lucifer.

Lucifer walks in circles,
With God forever present
And forever silent.

Goodbye Lucifer

Goodbye, Lucifer, goodbye:
I say goodbye to everything;
When the end arrives and knocks its time
My body won't dictate the tune
Nor my soul sing dead.
Goodbye, Utopia
Whose minute never came.
Goodbye –
In case I cannot say it then
Or death's too slow for me to care.

Goodbye, Lucifer, goodbye
People music language maps
Goodbye to love
And rivers alluvially curving.
Goodbye the sky.

Goodbye, Lucifer and all reflections,
Farewell to bodies and machinery
Goodbye the spirit of the universe
Goodbye.

Horse on Wenlock Edge

A tired horse treads
The moonpocked face
Of a ploughed field

Cuts furrows blindly
Through drifting rain
On chestnut trees, soaked hedges

Energy sucked out with evening;
Seven nails in each steel shoe
Are empty scars of twenty-eight nights

When the white horse dreams
Of galloping through star-clouds,
A moon of nails flying from its path.

Nottingham Castle

Clouds play with their water
Distort shekels between grass
Enriched by the city that flattens
Surrounding land with rubbish;

Binoculars ring the distance like a gun:
From a sea of shining slate
Churches lift and chimneys lurch,
Modern blocks block visions,

The Robin Hood Rifles drilled in fours
Practised azimuths on far-off points,
Eyes watering at southern hills
A half-day's march away:

'They'll have to swim the Trent, thou knows,
God-damn their goldfish eyes!'
Musket balls rush, break glass,
Make rammel. The Nottingham Lambs

Smashed more than a foreign army,
Came through twitchells to spark the rafters
Paint pillars with the soot of anarchy.
The Trent flowed in its scarlet coat

Too far off to deal with fire:
The council got our Castle in the end
Protected by Captain Albert Ball VC
Who thrust into a cloud-heap above Loos

Hoping for his forty-second kill.

In school they said: 'You're born
For Captain Albert Ball
To be remembered. Otherwise he'd die!'

A private soldier, he became Icarus:
'Dearest Folks, I'm back again
In my old hut. My garden's fine.
This morning I went up, attacked five Huns

Above the Line. Got one, and forced two down
But had to run, my ammunition gone.
Came back OK. Two hits on my machine.'
Fate mixed him to a concrete man

An angel overlooking
On the lawn of Nottingham's squat fort.
My memory on the terrace
Remembers barges on the Leen

Each sail a slice of paper, writing
Packed in script of tunic-red.
For eighteen years I blocked the view
No push to send me flying.

Another brain shot down in sleep:
Rich Master Robin Hood outside the walls
Where he belongs robs me of time
And does not give it to the poor.

The whimsical statue stood
With hat and Sherwood weapons
Till a Nottingham Lamb removed the arrow
Someone later nicked the bow

Then they stole the man himself
And rolled his statue down the hill
One football Saturday
And splashed it in the Trent:

If you see it moving, take it:
If it doesn't move, steal it bit by bit
But do not let it rest till Death's sonic boom
Blows the sun through every Castle room.

Oxney

Smoke all evening, too thin to move
Stubble aflame
Up a hillside when I drove
Across the flat half-mile between

Iden and the Isle of Oxney. A line
Of white, lipped in red set a corner
Of the battlefield on fire,
And cloud like a grey cloak was pulled along

By some heart-broken mourner going home.

North Star Rocket

At the North Pole everywhere is south.
Turn where you will
Polaris in eternal zenith
Studs the world's roof.

Under that ceiling
A grey rocket crosses
A continent of ice,
Evading Earth by flirting with it.

Who will know what planet he escaped from?
A cone of cosmic ash pursued its course
On automatic pilot set to earth

Bringing Death – or a new direction
To be fed into my brain
Before collision.

Fifth Avenue

A man plays bagpipes on Fifth Avenue.
Gaelic-wail stabbing at passersby
Who wish its pliant beckoning
Would draw them through their fence of discontent
To a field of freedom they can die in.
They stand, and then walk on.

A man with thick grey beard
Goes wild between traffic,
Arms wagging semaphore;
Raves warnings clear and loud
To those ignoring him.

A blind man rattles a money-can,
Dog flat between his legs
Listens to the demanding
Tin that has so little in
Both ears register
Each bit that falls.

An ambulance on a corner:
They put a man on a stretcher
Who wants air. A woman says:
'Is it a heart-attack?
Is the poor guy dead?'
She worries for him:
Dying is important when it comes.

'I suppose it is,' I guess,
'I hope it's not too late' –
She had one last year:

'Fell in the street, just like that.'
Her lips move with fear.
The man is slid into the van.

Just like that.
Hard to come and harder go
For the bagpipe player in the snow
The wild man with his traffic sport
The old man with his dog
And the young who hurry:
Dying, a lot of it goes on.

The Lady of Bapaume

There was a lady of Bapaume
Whose eyes were colourless and dead –
Until the falling sun turned red;
Her lovers from across the foam
Walked at dawn towards her bed:
Fell in fields and sunken lanes
Died in chalk-dust far from home.

A rash of scattered poppy-stains:
Nowadays they pass her wide –
That mistress of *chevaux-de-frise*
Is still alive and can't conceal
Her mournful and erotic zeal:
The lady of Bapaume had charms –
Bosom large, but minus arms.

No soldiers rise these days and go
Towards the bloodshot indigo.
Motorways veer by the place
On which, with neither love nor grace,
They drive to holidays in Spain.
There was a lady of Bapaume
Whose lovers ate the wind and rain.

Stones in Picardy

Names fade,
Suave air of Picardy erodes
The regimental badge
Or cross
Or David's Star
Of gunner this and private that.
The chosen captains and their bombardiers
And those known but as nothing unto God
Who brought them out of slime and clay
Are taken back again.

God knew each before they knew themselves
If ever they did
Before mothers lips sang
Brothers showed
Sisters taught
Fathers put them out to school or work.
But only God may know them when the stones are gone
If any can –
If God remembers what God once had done.

August

Birth, the first attack, begins at dawn.
It's also the last, whistle at sky-fall,
Illogical, unsynchronized, inept.
Children, pushed over the top
And kettledrummed across churned furrows
Kitted out with dreams and instinct,
Hope to learn before reaching the horizon.
Those in front call back advice:
'Going to advance, send reinforcements.'
But who trust the old, when they as young
Spurned cautionary wisdom
That never harmonized with youth?
'Going to a dance, send three-and-fourpence.'

Some fall quietly under each rabid burst of shell
Love of life unnoticed
In willingness to give it
Or the feckless letting-go.
Leaves drop in the zero-hour of spring
Young heat mangled by car or motorbike.

Broken sight looks in, no view beyond
Though terror rocks the heart to sleep
The signal-sky gives bad advice:
Get up, look outside, day again.
Insight warped by energy, blinded by ignorance.

The battlefield too wide,
Bullets rage at friends and parents
Strangers stunned in the lime-pits of oblivion.
Who blame for this sublime attack?

Did Brigadier-General God in his safe bunker plan?
He horsebacks by, devoted cheers.
Choleric face knows too much to tell –
It's dangerous for any smile to show.
Whoever is cursed must be believed in
For Baal is dead. Get up. Push on.
Want to live forever?
Go through. No psychic wound can split
Or leg be lost at that onrushing slope.

Halfway, more craven, sometimes too clever,
Old campaigners want a hole to flatten in
Before rot of the brain encircles
Or Death's concealed artillery
Plucks fingers from the final parapet.
Silence kills as quickly, you can bet.
Live on. Death pulls others in
Not you, or me, or us (not yet).

Earth underfoot is kind but waiting,
Green sea flows on the right flank,
Black rain foils the leftward sun,
Poppy clouds and mustard fields
Tricked out with dead ground, full woods,
Lateral valleys flecked with cornflowers.
Roses flake their fleshy petals down.
Time falls away. Battle deceptively recedes,
Peace lulls to the final killing ground,
Familiar voices coming up behind.

Moth

Drawn by the white glitter of a lamp
A slick-winged moth got in
My midnight room and ran quick
Around the switches of a radio.

Antennae searched the compact powerpacks
And built-in aerials, feet on metal paused
At METER-SELECT, MINIMUM-MAX
TUNER, VOLUME, TONE
Licked up shortwave stations onto neat
Click-buttons with precision feet.

Unable to forego the next examination
My own small private moth seemed all
Transistor-drunk on fellow-feeling,
A voluptuous discovery pulled
From some far bigger life.
A thin and minuscule antenna
Felt memory backtuning as it crawled
Familiar mechanism, remembering an instrument
Once cherished,
Forgotten but loved for old times' sake.

I switched the wireless on, and the moth
To prove its better senses
Mocked me with open wings and circled the light,
Making its own theatre, which outran all music.

Fishes

Fishes never change their habits:
A million years seem like a day
As far as fishes' habits go.

Beware of those who change them half as fast
Like people every year or so
So fast you cannot find
A firm limb or settled eye.

The constancy of fishes is unique.
They multiply but keep their habits
In deep and solitary state;

Feel unique and all alone
Not being touched and hardly touching
Even to keep the species spreading –
Unique is never-changing habits.

Fishes are flexible and fit the water,
And though continually moving
Never change their habits.

Release

Flowers wilt, leaves feloniously snatched,
Birds sucked away – autumn happens.
Frenetic bluebottles saw the air.
Blackberries scratch with poison.

Love is taken before knowing the mistake.
The last thief grins
At the look of life.
There are many, so who cares?

The trap is a loaded crossbow,
Ratchet-pulley sinewed back
From birth and set in wait.
None walk upright from the bolt's release.

Alioth the Bigot

A bigot walks fast.
Get out of the way
Or walk faster.

He walked faster too
Veered right
To evade me.

I increased my rate
Hinging left to avoid
The fire in his eyes.

Collisionable material
Should not promenade
On the same street.

We muttered sorry
Then went on
More speedily than ever.

On First Seeing Jerusalem

The way to knowing is to know
How useless to talk of hills and colours
Looking at Jerusalem.

To know is to keep silent
Yet in silence
One no longer knows;

Can never unknow what was known
Or let silence slaughter reason.
One knows, and always knows

Unable to believe silence
A better way of knowing.
One sees Jerusalem, knows

Yet does not, comes to life
And knows that walls outlast whoever watches.
The Temple was destroyed: one knows for sure.

One joins the multitude and grieves.
Knows it from within.
One does not know. Let me see you

Everyday as if for the first time
Then I'll know more:
Which already has been said

By wanderers who, coming home,
Regret the loss of that first vision.
The dust that knew it once is mute.

Stones that know stay warm and silent.
From pale dry hills I watch Jerusalem,
Make silence with the stones:
An ever-new arrival.

In Israel, Driving to the Dead Sea

I drive a car. Cars don't
Figure much in poems.
Poets do not like them,
Which is strange to me.

Poets do not make cars
Never have, not
One nut or bit of Plexiglass
Passes through their fingers.

No reason why they should.
To make a bolt or screw
Is not poetic. To fit a window:
Is that necessary?

Likewise an engine
Makes a noise. It smells,
And runs you off too fast.
What's more you have to sit

As fixed at work as that
Engine-slave who made it.
Nevertheless I drive a car
With pleasure. It makes my life poetic

I float along and tame
The road against all laws
Of nature. I stay alive.
Who says a poet shouldn't drive

On a highway which descends so low
Yet climbs so high
From Jerusalem to Jericho?

Receding Tide

The tide is fickle.
After going out it comes back.
The moon sees to that.

It's what the tide reveals
When it huffs and leaves
That means so much,

And what the tide covers
On nibbling back
That opens our eyes:

Archipelagos left unexplored
And rivers unsurveyed:
But before the meaning's known

The regimental rush of waves
Is preceded by
The brutal skirmishing of dreams.

Landscape – Sennen, Cornwall

How many died when the height was taken?
Upslope the armoured horses went:
Old refurbished iron-men
Zig-zagging from rocks,
And knights already fallen.

The cunning defenders
Jabbed soft underbellies,
Brought riders down
On gleaming daggers.

Victors mourned
As the defeated King rode
Into rain beyond the hill.

Blood makes history,
And desolation
A winter's day.

Derelict Bathing Cabins at Seaford

Well, they would, wouldn't they?
They'd say anything.
Doris and Betty got undressed.
Bob and Fred did the same next door.
The things that went on in these changing huts.
Well, with the War over, what could you expect?
They came back like new men.
Well, they came back.
They came, anyway.
Sometimes it was you and my Fred.
Then it might be me and your Bob.
It was nice with us, though, wasn't it?
Nothing but a clean bit of fun.
Sad they went in a year of each other –
The dirty devils!
Nothing but a clean bit of fun,
When we changed into our costumes,
The sea washed it off, though, didn't it?
We had some good swims as well.
And now look how they've smashed 'em up.
Poor old bathing huts.
Never be the same again.
The sea chucked all them pebbles in.
Don't suppose it liked the goings-on.
Then the vandals ripped the doors off.
They didn't like it, either.

Old times never come back,
But at least we 'ad 'em!

Derelict Houses at Whitechapel

We came off the ship:
'This is America. We're here!'
A shorter crossing
Than the railway trip.
Having to make a living
Was better than in Russia.
Nobody tried to kill us.

America was smaller than we thought.
We lived three generations
In those houses:
New Year
Atonement
Passover.

Bricks talk,
But Books are eloquent.

Window, Brighton

After thirty years he came home.
He had forgotten the house
But recognized the window.

His sister never married
But she knew he'd come.
They passed unknowing in The Lanes.

The first iron dewdrop of the knocker
Shook dust
From the flowers.

'Not today!' she said.
He walked away,
Forgot the house

Forgot the window
Forgot his sister never married
Forgot the knocker made no sound

When it struck home.

Torn Poster, Venice

The Big Voice, the Visual Scream
Shouts about the National Lottery
Or the advantage of travelling by Aeroflot
Or the holiness of the Virgin's Grotto
Or a film about the antics
At the court of King Otto;
Or did someone win
A Motto Competition –
First prize a reproduction
On a theme by Watteau?

Or, taking it all in all (and altogether)
Let's have a scenario like this:
The Big Bang Lottery Prize
Is a trip by Aeroflotto
To the Virgin's Grotto
In a corner of the Empire
Of mad King Otto –
From which you come back, if at all
(You've guessed it) BLOTTO;
Crossing the frontier in a haycart
Concealed inside the wrappings
Of a Cracker Motto
Against an idealized backdroppo
As designed by Watto.

Speculation is a dead-end,
So forget it. A mindless hand
A single rip: we'll never know
Where poster-dreams
And demons that lurk behind them go.

Early School

Claptrap, I said. Don't like this school.
Or probably much worse. If I'd learned
Nothing else I cursed like a sailor.
But five years old. Yet good, as good as gold.
They think I'm a fool?
Why am I here? They can say what they like.
They show me the swimming pool.
I get pushed in. It's cold.
My arms ache. I hold the bar,
Then aim for the other side. Not far.

Definitely don't like it. Suck my thumb.
Don't suck your thumb!
Scratch my nose. Don't do that!
She tells about The Wooden Horse of Troy.
Even I wouldn't have hauled that toy
Through the city walls like that.

She gives out bricks. We have to build.
Two suns blind her glasses.
Build, she says, build!
So I build a town. It gets knocked down.
Shall I throw them? Watch that frown.

She reads of Abraham from the Bible.
God says: Tie your son up on a pile of stones
Then slit his throat to show you love me most.
Isaac doesn't like it but his father
Lifts the knife. Just in time God tells him: Stop!
I believe you now, so drop the knife.

Make up your mind. Abraham cuts him free:
All that way for nothing.

My father did the same to me.
After school I longed to climb a tree.
But he held my hand
And at the bottom of the hill
He set me free.

Living Alone (For Three Months)

When you live alone
No goldfish or canary to adorn
The baffle between room and sky;
When you live alone –
Reveille out of bed at the alarm:
A dim pantechnicon of dreams
Darkens up the cul-de-sac of sleeping
Suddenly a flower of smithereens;
Do ten-minute jumps so that the heart
Won't burst at running for a bus:
Bathe;
Set breakfast: appetite's topography
Of battlefield hurdles, to infiltrate
And leap the parapet to wideawake;
Dump supper et cetera;
Then do your day;
And when dusk threatens
A fresh skirmishing of dreams
You (like a soldier between campaigns)
Devise a meal before lights-out
And bivouac –

When you live like such –
The person that you are turns two
Divides into a body and a voice
One moment stentor and the other glib
(Morality contending: talks
To the stack of flesh that cannot speak)
But only to hear the voice's tune
Flagging words both ears must listen to:

On the activating of what's gone
The switching on from plasmic and bewitching times
Where you thought yourself in love but weren't
Or when you said: I love, but didn't
Or would, but couldn't:
But no denying love's starlined coordinates
Crossing the heart of positively did:
The onrush, the complete positioning
Of being in love, and loved,
When the one same voice and body sang
The breath of passion into memory,
Into death via love –
The faces, her face, the truth
Of love that lasts forever but could not:
Yet giving life along the way
Through mist's uncertainties
Because it was and did.

Living by yourself, you talk,
Reshaping the heart
To fill the empty spaces
Out of spaces that you one time filled,
Making the alone-day,
Breaking the day like a stone.

Home

Landfall after the storm, going home through
White waves crumbling along the shore
Like piano keys pressed by invisible fingers,
Blue sky unfeeling what the sea does
To your boat, winds and subtle currents
Insidiously concerting.

Getting safe home through the storm
Provides no harbour or grandmother's face;
Waves turn you back as in a mirror breaking,
Each cliff falling on the soul
Like an animal with endless teeth.

Lancaster

At twenty-two he was an older man,
Done sixty raids and dropped 500 tons on target
Or near enough. Come for a ride, son:
Hi-di-hi and ho-di-ho, war over and be going soon.
He opened a map and showed the side that mattered,
Thumbed a line from Syerston to Harwell.

Our bomber shouldered up the runway
Cut the silver Trent in May:
Three years in factories
Made a decade out of each twelve-month,
From the cockpit viewing Southwell Minster
Under a continent of candyfloss,
Fields wheatened green recalling
Chaff blown and remaining corn
To soften in my sweetheart's mouth,
Then into a hedge and crush the dockleaves into
          greensmear.

The pilot banked his hundred wingspan south:
How much magnetic, how much true, how much
          compass –
Work the variation through,
Two hundred miles an hour and a following wind,
Harder to get home again over lace of roads and lanes
Plus or minus deviation for a course to steer
Red and black on spread map at the navigator's table,
A smell for life of petrol, peardrops and rexine.
Run a pencil down from A to B –
Now on the fortieth anniversary I reinvigorate
The game which formed my life's dead reckoning

Impossible to fathom as in that bomber I assumed I
      could –

Everything mechanical and easy to work,
Map in top-left pocket, crawling the long coffin
Between bombracks and centre section
No view of the world for forty feet,
Parachute forgotten but who goes back
At seventeen? Who thinks the air is not for him,
Merlin engines all his own, strip map beckoning
Through Death's cathedral for a dwarf?
Everything is there to open: the rear gunner's turret
For a technicolor backward view
A track made good of woods and the botch of
      Leicester
Railways of Rugby, the sandstone of Oxford
The peace of Abingdon and first view of the Thames,
Canals and rivers of new reality, calico tablecloth
Hiding all in me, unseen from my chosen seat.

Better not to know how I reached the far-back turret
Of downdraught and upcurrents, eyes on the past's
Wide fan shaping my destination.
A button put me side-on to the slipstream,
An east-west variation of the view. People ignored
The buzzing of our passage, engines hiding the silence
Of a so-far buried life, looking over four guns
Ready to suck all spirits up like fishes to a net.

Cherish the distance between them and me
But get inside the theatre of what goes on,
Or open the door and tumble into space –
No one would know I'd gone or where, destroying

The homely panorama and my body.
Death would not burn the spirit but I'd be off
And out of the map, shoes, tunic and cap looted
By gravity: Hello! as I spin, so glad to know you
But I never will. There, I don't belong,
My place forever looking down and in.

Alone, far back, to face the vanishing horizon squarely on.
Dim as it is, don't go, corrupted by haze
Loving what I cannot reach. The theatre's anatomy
And madness missed, don't care about a full cast
          waiting
To come in order of appearance and perform their
          dreams,
Ambition's engine, curtains holding back
Till the planet Lancaster divides the space
And I return over empty bombracks to get born again.

Delacroix's 'Liberty Guiding the People'

For the first few hundred yards
They knew her as a shirtmaker
Urging them over smoky corpses,
And when they said enough was enough
She climbed the lip of the barricade
To lead them over.

The world
Was impossible to open with a bayonet
That could not stop a cannon-ball in flight:
Nor could her red flag light them
Through a more than human darkness.

Then, whoever she was, she became LIBERTY.
No one knew when, by wonderful inspiration
She stripped off her shirt
And showed her bosom as a reminder
Of what brought them out of darkness.

Liberty, clothe your breasts
With that red flag –
I'll love you then.
Or let it guide the broken locomotive
Not the mob.

The boy with a pistol –
A cannon-ball took off his leg.
Your breasts gave liberty
But cured his worship.
Now he sells cheap pictures by the Louvre
Of *Mona Lisa* and *The Wreck of the Medusa*.

The Italian Woman

An Italian woman talking to her lover
On some far-off ocean
Mellifluously
From a villa in Liguria:
When are you coming back?
Shortwave static gruffed his voice.
I thought it would be soon, she said,
The scent of shrubs around her.

I love you, he said, but Neptune rules.
A sad laugh in her throat:
Yes, I understand,
So goodbye my handsome man,
I love you too.
The click of a telephone put down,
Sea noise rushing back.

Ah, love, I haven't lost you yet.
I love the sad laugh in her throat,
Face and body never to be seen
Nor flowers surrounding her.
I congratulate my rival,
And swing the needle onto other voices.

The Liberty Tree

First of all
The brambles had to be pulled out
By the roots.

With thick gardening gloves
Against the spikes
I burrowed around the tree bole

And clasped them tight
And tugged their stomachs
Out of cosy soil.

It wasn't enough.
I had to walk away
Dragging the whole entanglement

From topmost branches,
Evergreen needles snowing me
As claws protested.

I got them down.
And yanked them loose
But it was slow work

Then cut away the ivy
Broke each brittle snake-branch
From sucker tracks

Halfway up and round the trunk,
Some fingers
More tenacious than an arm.

Next it was the nettles' turn
Them I grasped low down;
The taller they were

The easier they came,
Bunches of stings
Cast out to die.

Every parasite has its protection
Stings or prickles
Growing in alliance,

Making it difficult to start.
At last it's done:
The tree no longer burdened.

Space cleared:
The beauty of its trunk revealed:
The biggest anaconda of them all.

A tree with space
Grows ten years in two,
Breathing sky unhindered,

Vibrations
Running through both hands to say:
People need freedom like a tree.

Noah's Ark

(On 12 January 1987, at 2230GMT, I took down an Italian news agency message in morse sent out specially to ships. The text said that Noah's Ark was no longer to be found on Mount Ararat, and gave details. The report originated in Tokyo, and the following lines are based on it.)

Earphones fed a message to the hand,
Hurried writing came through pat:
NOAH'S ARK IS NO LONGER FOUND ON MOUNT
ARARAT.

Words in Italian, sparks of Aaron's Rod
Rained across the page in morse
Like intelligence from God:
NOAH'S ARK IS NOT FOUND ON MOUNT ARARAT.

Morse flowed like splintered glass
The text unfinished, rattling on:
BUT IN ALL PROBABILITY YOU WILL FIND NOAH'S
ARK
ON A HILL FIVE HUNDRED METRES HIGH
ON THE BANKS OF THE TIGRIS BETWEEN SYRIA AND
TURKEY.

Rome International Radio informed all ships
Swaying the emerald Atlantic waves
Urgent news of Ararat,
And Marconi operators wrote the gen
And typed it with the morning news,
Sailors with shocked eyes and lips atremble said:
L'ARCA DI NOÈ NON SI TROVA SUL MONTE ARARAT!

Perhaps Noah's Ark had been not lost
But one dark night dissected
And put on donkeys for a secret destination.
Hot-footed morse did not originate from God:
A Japanese expedition from an Electronics Firm
Led by YOSHIO KOU had combed
The scrub of Chaldees with a Bible and a map
Finally concluding that
NOAH'S ARK IS NO LONGER ON MOUNT ARARAT

Kids at school threw down their pens
Church and Synagogue were worried
And the Zurich bourse was flurried.
But fact and inspiration tell
How the Ark came on to Ararat because
The navigation of the Pilot was spot-on.
A dove and olive twig to guide the rudder:
And travelling all night above Lake Van
The snowy light was not one cloud of many
But glinting Araratic glaciers in the dawn.

Anchored by a terminal moraine
Noah ordered animals and humans to disperse.
God camouflaged the Ark from archaeologists
Who scour the land with lamp and map.
What YOSHIO KOU found by the Tigris
Was not an Ark but a canoe,
Though matters Biblical led him to state
NOAH'S ARK IS NO LONGER BEACHED ON ARARAT.

The story in the Bible's better:
Of how the Ark on Day Seventeen
After the flood that God begat

Bumped against the banks of Ararat.

The Ark, in spite of YOSHIO KOU, lies under rocks
On tufic Ararat, below a Turkish post
That looks on Persia.
I saw it in a dream, and sent a message back
By telegraphic key
Feet tapping to its rhythm on the mat:
NOAH'S ARK'S STILL HIDDEN ON MOUNT ARARAT.